Your
Humble
Prayee

After insuring taxes are paid, 100% of author's proceeds from "Your Humble Prayee" are contributed to charity.' In prayer, distribution of book should proceed with Christians of greatest responsibility over Christians, simultaneously by denomination, eventually reaching bookstores.

Balboa Press books may be ordered through booksellers or by contacting:

Balboa Press
A Division of Hay House
1663 Liberty Drive
Bloomington, IN 47403
www.balboapress.com
844-682-1282

ISBN: 978-1-9822-1727-3 (sc)
ISBN: 978-1-9822-1726-6 (e)

Print information available on the last page.

Balboa Press rev. date: 03/30/2021

Dedicated to the intent of unity of Christian faith across all denominations, the expectations of Jesus, fulfillment left to God.

BALBOA.PRESS
A DIVISION OF HAY HOUSE

Your Humble Prayee

Faithfulness Forever

- ➤ " 'In humble Loving Prayer for Peace through: **H**oliness of **S**pirit,
  To: *O*ur **H**oly Mediator **L**ord **J**esus,
  For: **G**od *O*ur **F**ather and **C**reator of all (including opportunity of prayer)**,** Hallowed be
  Your <u>most</u> **H**oly name Jehovah -- which, as three, art as *O*ur **B**lessing in Heaven;

- ➤ **Y**our Kingdom come: Intent on earth be done as it is kept in Heaven;

- ➤ All Praise be to **G**od **W**hom: Gives *U*s daily cares, Loves *U*s forever,
  Wisens *U*s against abuse of the harmful**,** Keeps *O*ur **F**amilies united,
  Opportunities *U*s with an initial* precious opposite gendered spousal Love,
  Instills instinct in *U*s from wrongful temptation, Stresses to *U*s importance of
  Forgiveness,
  while Everlasting the submergely <u>*B*</u>aptized in **L**ordly Faith from evil;

- ➤ Whose will is: The **K**ingdom, **P**ower and **G**lory forever and ever be**,**
  Interim goaling *U*s to make Christian *D*isciples of all Nations,
  Then, all Authority be to **C**hrist *O*ur Councilor**,** in **J**esus' name**,** amen. ' "

Your Humble Prayee

Generic Adolescent's Prayer

Thank You God for blessing.
May You extend blesses to:

- The Church, Holy Bible and instinct to pray,
- Our US President and all elected officials,
- Teachers and fellow students,
- Parents, family, and friends,
- Police, fire department and rescue workers,
- Gifts of beneficial imagination, love, kindness, respect, good health and self-control,
- Concepts of teamwork, direction, guidance, sharing, compassion and forgiveness,
- Fond memories of special times: Birthdays, holidays and vacations,
- And lastly, especially Jesus, for being all mine, check that—Ours.

PS - Responsibilities of courtesy, chores, pet care, homework, tests, wage earning, career selection and <u>safe</u> vehicle driving & dating.

In Jesus' name, Amen.

Your Humble Prayee

Humbly to Dear Beloved God in Heaven

> ➢ Please give us a president who loves this country and everything it stands for.
>
> ➢ Please give us a president who respects You and loves You as the one true God.
>
> ➢ Please give us a president who will, with Your help, restore this nation to its former glory, the way You created her.
>
> ➢ Please help us to respect what You have given to us and not take anything for certainty ever again.
>
> ➢ Please God, weaken the evil and strengthen the good, both within and without.
>
> May our eyes and hearts of voter understanding be opened.
>
> All glory to God, In Jesus' name,
>
> Amen

Your Humble Prayee

Generic empathic prayer for Election Day

1. Please give us elected officials who love this country and everything it stands for.
2. Please give us elected officials that respect You and love You as the one true God.
3. Please give us elected officials who will, with Your help, restore this nation to its former glory, the way you created her.

4. Please help us respect what You have given to us and not take anything for certainty again.
5. Please God, weaken the evil and strengthen the good, both within and without.

6. May our eyes, minds and hearts of voter understanding be opened.
7. All Glory to God, in Jesus' name. Amen.

P. S. - May God's Son bless all who contributed their time to make this election possible!

Your Humble Prayee

An empathic prayer for all requiring surgery:
May they (in order):

1. Keep faith in God through Jesus Christ,
2. Completely trust in those chosen to heal,
3. Possess enough strength to endure,
4. Be granted enough time to completely recover,
5. Then, filled with the Holy Spirit, reveal a zest for life and desire to pray.

In Jesus' name, amen.

Your Humble Prayee

An empathic prayer for any Church appointing new or renewed leadership:

May the new leadership (in order):

1. Keep faith in God through Jesus Christ,
2. Always pray through Jesus for God's will to prevail,
3. Humbly cherish as exemplary, the specific scripture required to hold office,
4. Then, filled with the Holy Spirit, serve the office as wisely and gratefully as your experience permits.

In Jesus' name, amen.

Your Humble Prayee

An empathic prayer for all requiring special care:
May they (in order);

> 1. Keep faith in God through Jesus Christ,
> 2. Completely trust in those providing care,
> 3. Possess a heart that cherishes friendships,
> 4. Being filled with the Holy Spirit, reveal a zest for life, and desire to pray.

P.S. In prayer, may God's Son bless our caregivers with love, patience and understanding.

In Jesus' name we pray, amen.

Your Humble Prayee

Faithfulness Forever

> ➤ " 'In humble Loving Prayer for Peaceful Innocence through: **H**oliness of **S**pirit, To: **J**esus - *O*ur **H**oly **G**race mediator, Salvation authority and Sincerity **D**ivine, For: **Y**our **F**ather **G**od - **C**reator of all (including opportunity of prayer), Hallowed be **H**is <u>most</u> **H**oly name **J**ehovah -- which, as **T**hree, art as *O*ur **B**lessing in Heaven;
>
> ➤ Theory of Kingdom come: Intent on earth be done as it is kept in Heaven;
>
> ➤ All Praise be to **Y**our **F**ather **W**hom: Gives *U*s daily cares, Loves *U*s forever, Wisens *U*s against abuse of the harmful, Keeps *O*ur **F**amilies united, Opportunities *U*s with an initial precious opposite gendered spousal Love, Instills instinct in *U*s from wrongful temptation, Stresses to *U*s importance of Forgiveness, while Everlasting the submergely <u>*B*</u>aptized in **L**ordly Faith with Heaven;
>
> ➤ **W**hose realms are: The **A**uthority, **P**ower and **G**lory forever and ever be, **and** For *U*s to make Christian *D*isciples of all *N*ations, **then,** <u>all</u> Rewarding be to **J**esus, *O*ur **L**ord and **M**essiah,
>
> *We* pray in the name of **J**esus, amen.' "

"Improving Prayer - For reader comparison"

Your Humble Prayee

Generic Adolescent's Prayer:

Thank You God for blessing and understanding.
May You extend blesses to:

➤ Your Churches, Holy Bible and instinct to pray,

➤ Our US President and all elected officials,

➤ Principals, teachers and fellow students,

➤ Parents, family, and friends,

➤ Police, fire department, rescue workers, health officials and hope for judges,

➤ Gifts of beneficial imagination, love, kindness, respect, good health and self-control,

➤ Concepts of teamwork, direction, guidance, sharing, compassion and forgiveness,

➤ Fond memories of special times: Birthdays, holidays and vacations,

➤ Jesus especially, all His believers and Self for defense of our destiny from enemies.

PS - Also responsibilities of courtesy, chores, pet care, homework, tests, wage earning, career selection and **safe** vehicle driving & dating.

In Jesus' name we pray, Amen.

"Improving Prayer - For reader comparison"

Your Humble Prayee

Printed in the United States
by Baker & Taylor Publisher Services